Contents

Material Wealth

Fibres and Threads

Human beings have always made use of easily-available natural resources for making materials. Animals like sheep and goats provide fleece and hair for wool. Skins for leather also come from animals. Silk comes from the silkworm. Plants give us fibres, like cotton and linen, that can be spun and woven into cloth.

To produce a new fabric usually means using up natural resources to supply and make the yarn. These natural resources can never be replaced. By re-using rags and remnants you can help conserve the Earth's energy resources. You can also reduce the size of local landfill sites, by recycling old garments.

Recycling Fabrics

Poverty has always forced people to re-use or recycle clothing and cloth remnants. In some developing countries often the only available materials are discarded items. Today it is essential that every one of us should make the best use of all such materials as the Earth's natural resources are fast disappearing.

Litter accumulates in places the world over. Four per cent of this is old clothing. By sorting this waste into recyclable and non-recyclable groups of materials, we can use many of our throwaway items again. Recycled nylon waste, for example, can be made into tennis balls and old garments into carpet underlay.

Local people sort rubbish on a tip in Bangkok, Thailand, to collect together items that can be re-used or recycled.

ART FROM FABRIC

with projects using rags, old clothing and remnants

Gillian Chapman & Pam Robson

WAYLAND

Art from Fabric
Art from Packaging
Art from Paper
Art from Rocks and Shells
Art from Sand and Earth
Art from Wood

This book was prepared for Wayland (Publishers) Ltd
by Globe Education, Nantwich, Cheshire
Artwork and design by Gillian Chapman
Photography by Rupert Horrox

First published in 1995 by Wayland (Publishers) Ltd

This paperback edition published in 2005 by Hodder Wayland,
an imprint of Hodder Children's Books

Reprinted in 2006 by Wayland, an imprint of Hachette Children's Books

Printed in China

British Library Cataloguing in Publication Data
Chapman, Gillian
Art from Fabric. – (Salvaged series)
I. Title. II. Robson, Pam. III. Series
746

ISBN-10: 0 7502 4781 9
ISBN-13: 978 0 7502 4781 8

Picture Acknowledgments
Ecoscene 4t (Ian Beames);
Eye Ubiquitous 4b (John Hulme); Link 5b (Orde Eliason)
Zefa 5t

Wayland
an imprint of Hachette Children's Books
338 Euston Road, London NW1 3BH

*Ninety-five per cent of the materials used for the projects
in this book were salvaged scraps and remnants*

Collecting

For the projects in this book, you can seek out remnants of fabric at jumble sales and charity shops. Look around at home and select any old clothing or household fabrics. Make sure you use only clean materials. Remove any buttons or zips, as these can be re-used. Woollen items can be unravelled. Small scraps of cloth are useful for collage, appliqué or patchwork.

Small remnants of fabric are sewn together to make patchwork quilts. Designs are often traditional.

A scarecrow made from cast-off clothing and fabric remnants. This scarecrow was used to protect crops in a field in southern Africa.

New from Old

Today there is a great demand for the work of craftspeople who rely upon recycled objects and materials for inspiration. Creativity depends upon the resources available. It is possible to create beauty out of waste.

Quilts known as khols are made from chindi – rags collected and sorted by the poor in India. In Bangladesh, quilts known as kanthas were traditionally made from scraps and unpicked threads of worn-out saris and dhotis. A kantha is often given as a wedding gift.

In Thailand, scraps of cloth are used to make oven gloves and toys. Silk cocoons are dyed and shaped into flowers. A slipper-sock knitting project employs hundreds of refugees in Pakistan, using unravelled wool from second-hand knitted garments. Cotton scraps are used to make Indian festival decorations. Cotton rags can be used to make paper.

Shifting Shapes

Shape and Size

When you collect together discarded fabrics and clothing you will find a variety of small decorative items and fasteners, like buttons, beads and buckles, that can be removed. Look at their different shapes. Some will be curved, others will be angular. They will be made from a range of materials – coloured plastic buttons, metal zips and fasteners, wooden and glass beads. Sizes will vary from enormous to tiny, depending upon the garments that they have been taken from.

Colour Wheel

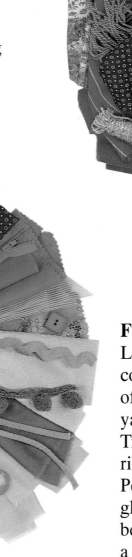

A Typical Collection of Discarded Fabrics and Trimmings

Fabric Colour Wheel

Look carefully at all the items in your collection. You have probably found lots of different fabric remnants – scraps of yarn, patches of denim and pieces of felt. Trimmings may include lace, cords, ribbons, tapes and old shoe laces. Perhaps you have found an odd sock or glove, or an old belt buckle. You can begin by organizing your collection into a colour wheel.

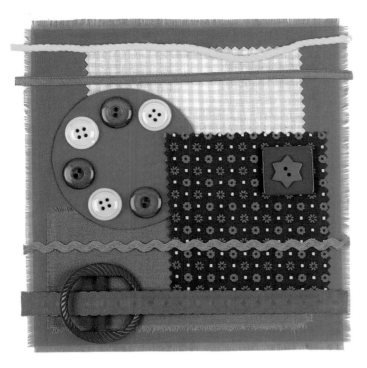

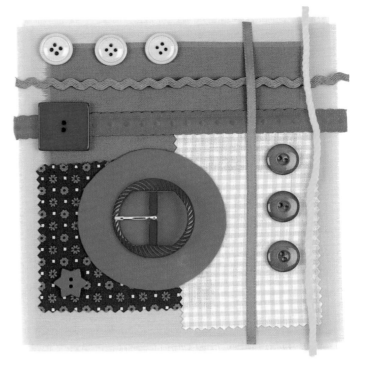

Moving Patterns

Now arrange some of the items to create a temporary collage. Move the objects about until you find the arrangement that you like best. You will discover many interesting ways to position the same articles.

Shifting Shapes

Make a series of arrangements, using background materials of different colours and textures. Take a photograph, or sketch each one before rearranging.

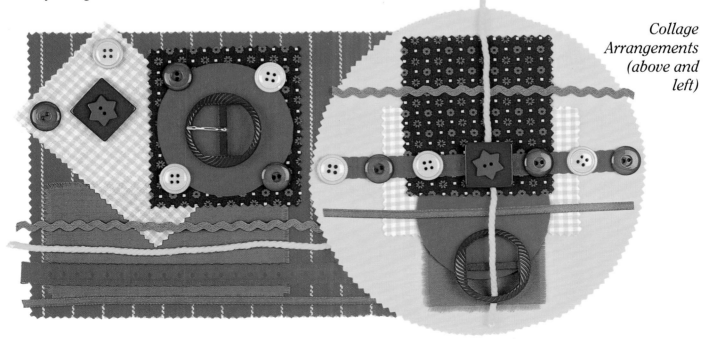

Collage Arrangements (above and left)

7

Fabric Collages

Colour and Texture

All fabrics, whether they are natural or manufactured, have their own special properties. Silk is lightweight and smooth to the touch, while wool feels rough. Woven silk fabric is shiny. Woollen cloth has a matt finish and is used to make garments to keep us warm. Feel the fabrics in your collection – which are rough and which are smooth? Look at them – which are shiny and which are matt?

Woven or Non-Woven

Most fabrics are woven on a loom, but there are some that are non-woven. Felt is made by compression using heat and moisture. A non-woven fabric will not fray. Fabrics that fray easily can be difficult to use. For a fabric collage try to choose materials like felt. Some fabrics, like hessian, are loosely woven and are hard and stiff. Other woven fabrics, like polyester, a manufactured fabric, are soft and delicate.

Underwater Collage

Fabric Collage

Make a fabric collage using as many coloured, textured materials as you can. Plan out the design first by sketching a picture the same size as your finished collage. Cut your sketch into separate parts to use as patterns. Find a large piece of strong fabric or card backing. You may decide to glue your collage to the backing cloth or sew the pieces into place.

Arrange the collage pieces following your sketch. If your picture is a landscape or an underwater scene choose fabrics suited to the subject. Overlap silky materials and netting. Fray and ripple the fabric to create a wavy effect. If you have yarns, trimmings and buttons that match your colour scheme use them for details.

You can create an abstract collage by arranging the fabrics according to colour or texture. Place warm or cool colours together or grade them from light to dark.

Colour Collage
(right)

Extra Collage
Materials

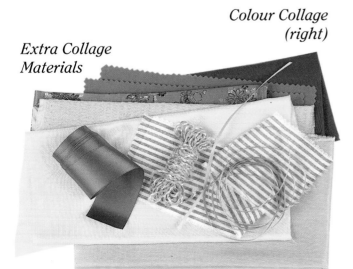

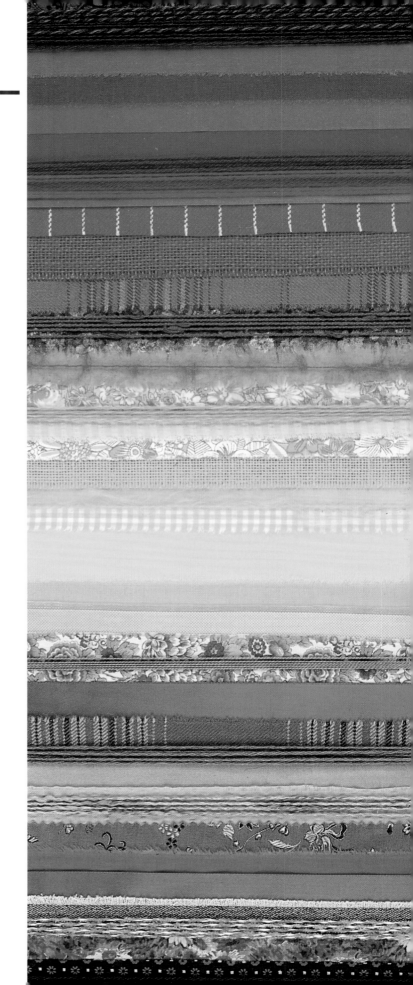

Woven Threads

Spiders' Webs

Spiders are skilled at weaving. The ancient Greek story of Arachne tells how she and the goddess Athena took part in a weaving competition. Arachne was turned into a spider by the jealous Athena because her weaving was the best. Scientists wishing to make lightweight fabric strong enough to withstand bullets, are experimenting with genetic engineering using spiders' silk genes.

Warp and Weft

Warp threads lie lengthwise along a roll of cloth. They are the downward threads on a loom. Weft threads are woven in and out across the downward warp threads. Stretchy warp threads are best because they must be pulled taut. Threads that do not stretch will snap under tension.

Looms

Weavers work on a frame called a loom. Materials woven on a loom are many and varied, particularly woollen cloth. Many woollen goods have a fluffy surface because the fibres lie in all directions. Worsted cloth is smooth as the woollen fibres are combed parallel.

Collecting Threads

Make a collection of different threads pulled from a variety of fabrics and materials. See if you can identify them. Are they wool, cotton, linen or polyester? Are they synthetic or natural? Find a piece of loosely woven fabric, such as hessian or sacking. Carefully pull out a number of the weft threads. Weave threads from your collection into the sacking to make a colourful new fabric.

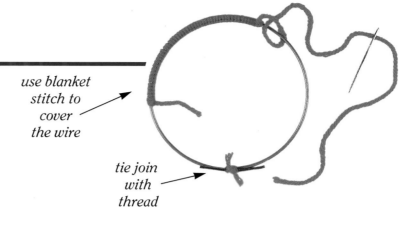

use blanket stitch to cover the wire

tie join with thread

Making a Sun Burst

A simple loom can be made by bending a wire coat hanger into a circle. Overlap the ends and tie the join with thread. Cover the wire loop with long threads or narrow strips of fabric. Tie threads across the circle and weave other threads in and out, as shown here. Use different textures and thicknesses to create a colourful effect. Finally decorate the Sun Burst with trimmings, such as buttons, beads and feathers and hang it up.

Finished Sun Bursts

Weaving Threads (left)

11

Working with Yarns

Weaving Traditions

In Africa, weaving traditions vary considerably. In North Africa, it is the women who do the weaving. In West Africa and East Africa, it is more likely to be the men. Many different types of looms are used. Today, traditional cloths are being replaced by factory-produced fabrics.

Kente cloth, woven from strips of rayon or silk, made by the Asante peoples of Ghana, was once made only for kings. In Malaysia, Songket cloth weaving is an ancient craft. Traditional patterns are woven in gold and silver threads. The finished cloth is worn by Malaysians on ceremonial occasions.

Unravelling Hand Knits

Unravelling Yarn

Unwanted knitted garments can easily be taken to pieces. The unravelled yarn is crinkly and this can give an interesting texture to your projects. Choose only clean hand knits, in good condition. Wind the different yarns on to card bobbins, separating the colours. You can use this yarn for a weaving project.

Making Pom-Poms

These yarns can also be used to make colourful pom-poms. To make a pom-pom cut two card circles the same size. Cut a hole in the centre of both circles. Wind the yarn through the two rings until the centre hole is full. Carefully cut the wound yarn at the edge of the card. Tie strong thread between the rings and knot it tightly before cutting the cards to remove them.

cutting

card shape

winding

Making Pom-Poms

Winding Yarn

In Guatemala, scraps of bright coloured cottons are woven into animalitos – small animals. Here is an idea for winding yarn scraps around pieces of card to make these animal pictures.

You will need a piece of thick card and a selection of yarns. Make small notches in the sides of the card to secure the ends of each length of wool. Wind the yarn around the card, choosing different colours and textures to create a striped effect.

Find a piece of fabric the same size as the card and cut an animal shape from the centre. Place the fabric over the top of the weaving so that the coloured stripes are visible through the animal-shaped hole. Sew or glue the fabric frame to the card.

Winding Wool on to Cards

Elephant Stencil Made from Fabric

Finished Elephant Picture

Add fabric features such as ears.

Decorate the fabric with coloured stitching.

13

Flying Fish

Fishes and Dragons

Windsocks were used by Roman soldiers to find out wind strength and direction for their archers and also to frighten the enemy. In 1066 when the Normans invaded Britain, the Anglo-Saxon banner was a dragon-shaped windsock. Historians think this is so because it can be seen on the Bayeux Tapestry.

In Japan, the Boys' Festival is celebrated on the fifth day of the fifth month. Families with male children fly a brightly coloured windsock from the roof. The most popular shape is the carp. This fish struggles to swim upstream each year and symbolizes the boy's journey through life.

Making a Carp Windsock

basic carp shape

Cut out two basic carp shapes and sew them together.

Lightweight Materials

A windsock must blow easily in the wind and should be made from durable, lightweight materials. Synthetic fabrics like nylon and polyester have these properties. Old sheets, shirts and petticoats are most suitable for the purpose.

To make a windsock you will need a large piece of fabric, such as a nylon sheet, and smaller scraps of coloured material for decoration. The windsock acts as a wind tunnel, open at both ends. Look at pictures of traditional Japanese windsocks. Use these to sketch out your design.

Cutting out the Shape

Follow your design and cut out two body shapes from the sheeting. Pin and sew them together.

tail opening

mouth → opening

14

Making a Windsock

Make a hem in the mouth opening through which to thread a length of coat hanger wire. Twist the two ends of the wire together to make a loop. This will keep the mouth open.

Decorate the windsock by glueing or sewing pieces of material to the body. Overlap circle shapes for scales and make pleated fins and a tail.

Tie three lengths of cord to the wire loop and attach these securely to a strong stick. Now find a high and exposed place to fix your windsock.

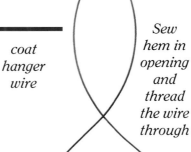

coat hanger wire

Sew hem in opening and thread the wire through

Making the Mouth

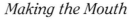

Fabric Circles and Pleats for Decoration

Finished Carp Windsock

15

Swooping Snakes

Chinese Kites

Kites existed in China as early as the fifth century BC. They were flown for both pleasure and for military purposes. Kites shaped like mythical birds and dragons were common. Many had rolling eyes and moving tails. Some whistled as they flew and were used to frighten enemies. Kite flying did not reach Europe until the sixteenth century.

Materials for Kites

A kite must be light and manageable. It must also be strong. The materials to make a kite need to be lightweight and durable. In ancient times, the Chinese used silk or paper for their kites but paper is not durable. Today synthetic fabrics like nylon and polyester can be used.

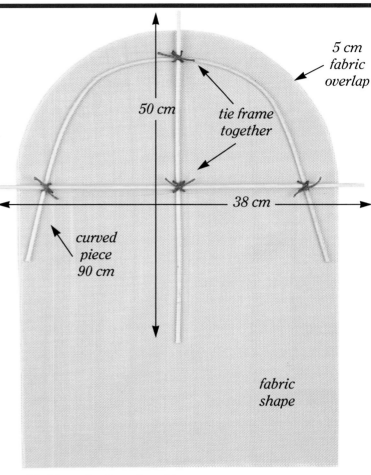

50 cm

5 cm fabric overlap

tie frame together

38 cm

curved piece 90 cm

fabric shape

Making the Bamboo Frame

Attaching Fabric to the Frame

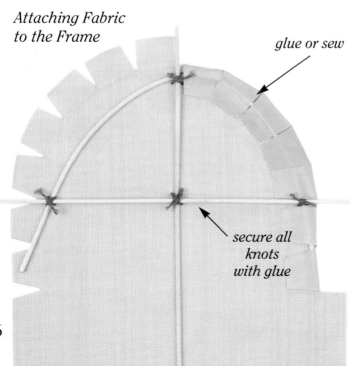

glue or sew

secure all knots with glue

A Snake Kite

This snake kite is simple to make. Because of its flat head and long tail it can fly in the lightest breeze. Choose lightweight materials to make the kite and decorate it with scraps of coloured fabric or paper.

Making the Frame

The frame is made from three pieces of flexible bamboo which are cut to the following sizes: 1 x 50 cm, 1 x 38 cm and 1 x 90 cm. Assemble the frame by tying the pieces together as shown in the diagram above.

Attaching the Body

Choose a large piece of strong, lightweight fabric for the head. It will need to be larger than the bamboo frame. Place the frame on top of the fabric, as shown opposite. Cut the fabric to the shape of the frame leaving a 5 cm overlap all round. Glue or sew the fabric to the frame. Secure all knots and bindings with blobs of glue to make them extra strong.

Overlap fabric circles for the tail.

Finished Snake Kite

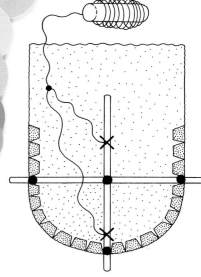

Attaching the Strings

Making the Tail

The tail is made from overlapping circles of fabric or paper. Begin by glueing them to the head and extend the kite by making the tail as long as you like.

Rigging the Strings

It is important to make sure the strings are balanced and attached firmly to the kite. Use a strong nylon thread and follow the stringing diagram above.

Take care when you fly your snake kite. Make sure an adult is nearby and you do not stand close to overhead power lines or trees.

Glove Puppets

Traditional Puppets

Puppeteering is an ancient skill common to many cultures. The oldest type of puppeteering began in India where rod and hand puppet performances were popular forms of entertainment. Hand puppets are perhaps the simplest to make and the easiest to operate. They are often found in countries that have strong traditions of storytelling, where they are used to bring a story to life.

Materials for Hand Puppets

Marking the Position of Features

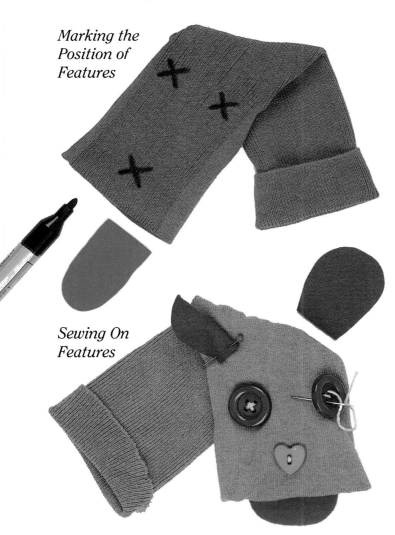

Sewing On Features

Making Hand Puppets

If you have odd socks, mittens and gloves amongst your collection of oddments they can be turned into puppet characters.

Place your hand inside a sock with your fingers in the toe and thumb in the heel. Push in the sole of the sock to form the puppet's mouth. Using a black felt pen, mark where the eyes, nose and ears should be positioned.

Cut out ears and a tongue from scraps of fabric and sew them into place. Use buttons and beads for the nose and eyes.

Other Ideas

Odd gloves and mittens can also be made into puppets. Push in the middle fingers and thumb of an old glove. Stuff the first and little finger with small fabric scraps to make ears for your puppet, then add the other features.

Use Old Gloves and Mittens

Making a Puppet Theatre

To make a puppet theatre, find a strong cardboard box, large enough for the puppets to move inside. Cut a hole in the front of the box for the stage. Operate the puppets through a smaller hole cut from the back.

Decorating the Theatre

Cover the box with material and decorate it with fabric scraps and trimmings. Make some curtains and scenery, attaching them to the inside of the theatre. Write a short play for all your hand puppet characters.

Puppet Theatre

19

Performing Puppets

Giant Puppets

The largest string puppets originated in Japan. They are called Bunraku and need two or three people to operate them. It takes many years for the operators to master their art. Smaller string puppets are sometimes called marionettes. The strings are attached to a small wooden frame. The puppeteer remains hidden from view whilst operating the puppets. There may be as many as nine strings to work. It is a very skilled job, requiring careful concentration.

Puppet Bodies

A string puppet must have a firm, but flexible body. Think about the materials you are using – they must be light, but strong. Choose a suitable piece of fabric for the body and attach lengths of yarn or cord. These form the arms and legs. Thread large, heavy buttons to the ends of the strings for hands and feet. For the head shape, either stuff nylon tights with cotton wool, or make a woollen pom-pom (see page 12). Sew the head to the fabric body.

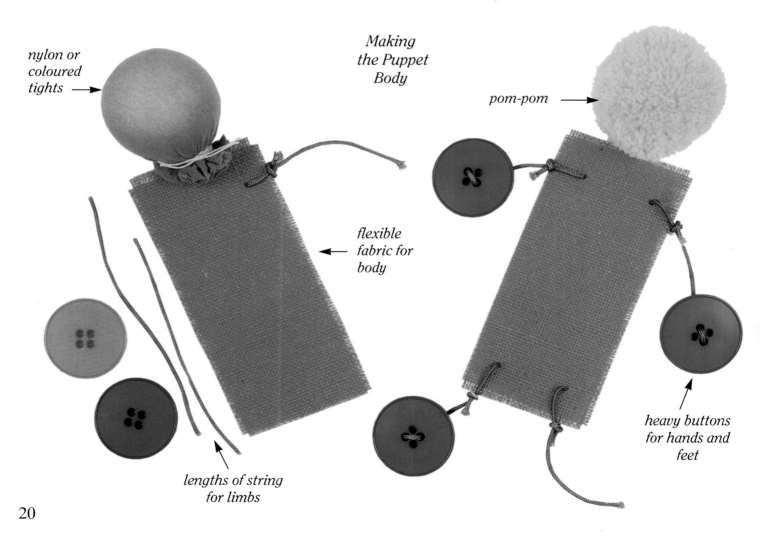

nylon or coloured tights →

Making the Puppet Body

pom-pom →

flexible fabric for body ←

lengths of string for limbs

heavy buttons for hands and feet

Creating a Character

Once you have made the basic puppet shape you can decorate it in many ways to turn it into a character. Use material to cover the body and limbs, glueing or sewing them together. Be careful not to make the puppet too stiff – it must always move freely. If you have fabric remnants, wool scraps, buttons and trimmings use them imaginatively to create your character.

Cat and Mouse Characters

Control Bar made from Lollipop Sticks

Attaching the Strings

Use a string that is lightweight, but strong. The puppet will need strings attached to all four limbs and one supporting string from the head. Thread strings through the button hands and feet, and sew one to the top of the head. Make sure you have the correct lengths before trimming them. Attach them to a control bar, like the one shown above.

mouse

cat

Rag Rugs

Collecting Rags

In India, particularly in Ahmedabad in Gujarat, women and children collect and sort rags or chindi to provide material for the textile industry. The rags are recycled to make artefacts such as rag rugs for the local market and for export. Varanasi is well known for its rag rug industry. The rug makers mostly work in their homes using panja looms.

The traditions of rag rug making are international, but all are based on the common idea 'waste not, want not'. Even scraps of fabric that are too small for practical use can be recycled.

Planning a Rag Rug

You will need to collect together a large quantity of different fabrics to make a rug, so start by making a smaller mat to practise. Sort the fabrics into type and colour and make sure they are all clean. Separate plain and patterned materials and discard any that are too thick. Fine cotton and synthetic fabrics are ideal.

Begin by cutting or tearing the fabrics into long strips. You will be plaiting three strips together to make long braids which will then be coiled and sewn together to make the mat. Think about the colour scheme of the finished mat. You may use light colours at the centre and darker shades around the edge.

Plaiting

C

B

A

To plait a braid, place the left strip A over the centre one B. Then place strip C over A. Repeat these moves until all the fabric is used

Different Plaited Effects

Plaiting Braids

Lay the three lengths of fabric on a flat surface and begin plaiting them together, as shown opposite. Use a mixture of coloured and patterned lengths to make different effects. Make a number of these braids, until you use up all the fabric.

Coiling and Sewing

The mat is made by coiling the plaited braids into a circular or oval shape and sewing them into place with strong thread. As the lengths of braid are wound around, new lengths are pinned and sewn in, as shown here. Continue until the mat is finished.

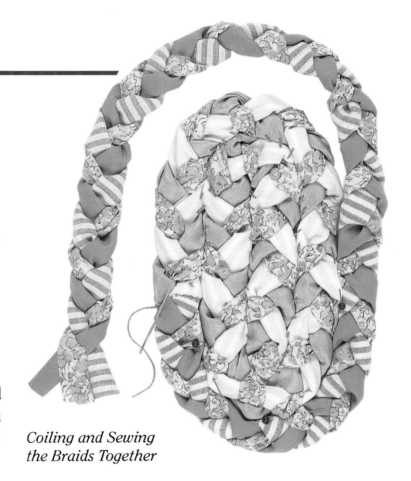

Coiling and Sewing the Braids Together

Finished Coiled Rag Rug

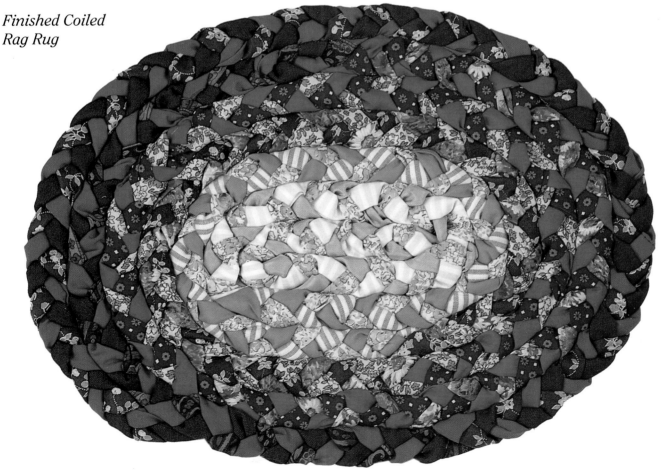

Rag Books

The Meaning of Patchwork

In some societies the use of discarded items to create something whole has a religious significance. Both Hindus and Buddhists see the patching of cloth as an act of humility. Raffia dance skirts worn by the Kuba women of Africa were often patched. These comma-shaped patches were then turned into a design known as 'shina mboa' – the tail of the dog. In America, patchwork patterns are given names, like Ohio Star. Amish quilts have striking abstract designs.

A Picture of the Past

Articles of clothing can remind us of people and past events. You may look at an old item of clothing and remember the occasion on which it was worn. It might have been a wedding or a birthday celebration. Gather together scraps of fabric taken from such garments and piece them together to create a patchwork history of your family. Design a picture in the form of a family tree. Choose suitable material and make a patch for each member of the family.

Patchwork Family Tree

youngest generation at the top

A Patchwork Story

You can make a patchwork story book from your collection. Use pieces of household fabrics, like old curtain or upholstery material, to make the pages of the book. Sew them together using a running stitch. Choose fabrics that remind you of a particular house or room.

Collect scraps of fabric from old clothing belonging to your family. Some of them may have special memories and stories attached to them. Make patch pockets from these pieces of fabric and sew them into the book. Write about the fabrics and the people associated with them and put the stories, with any photographs, inside.

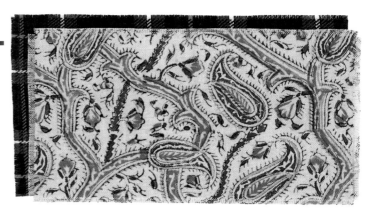

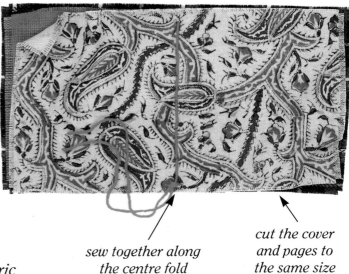

Making a Book from Fabric

sew together along the centre fold

cut the cover and pages to the same size

patch pockets containing stories and photographs

label for the title

My Family

My Home

25

New Clothes from Old

Fashionable Clothes

The fashion world is becoming more conscious of the environment. Some designers are choosing fibres like cotton only if they have been grown without the use of pesticides. The finished clothes are expensive, but changes are coming. Tencel is a new fabric that is a mixture of wood pulp and cotton. Remnants of cotton are recycled and turned into paper.

Patching to Create a New Fabric

Patchwork Hat

Patchwork Bag

Fashionable Patching

Hard times make it necessary to patch and mend clothes. Nowadays, it is common practice to patch the elbows and knees, even on new garments, to prevent wear and tear. Sometimes a patchwork effect is used on clothes and bags because it is fashionable.

Look through your collection of materials and make a new fabric by sewing pieces together. Design and make something useful. Keep your ideas simple and make a paper pattern first as a reference.

Weaving Ties

New and exciting fabrics can be made by weaving old and unwanted items together. Ties very quickly become unfashionable and as a result are discarded. Collect together as many colourful, silky ties as you can find. Weave them together to make a brand new fabric.

*Weaving
Old Ties*

*Trainer
Book-Ends*

Trainer Book-ends

It is difficult to know what to do with old trainers and shoes that are worn out or too small. Wash them and then try painting them with acrylic paints. Fill them with stones or plaster to make them heavy and turn them into book-ends.

AHLBERG LE GENTIL FACTEUR ALBIN MICHEL JEUNESSE

AH, VOUS DIRAI-JE MAMAN nathan

Rag Dolls

Ancient Dolls

Examples of the first rag dolls can still be seen in museums today. One doll that was found in Egypt has been made from a coarse fabric and stuffed with rags.

African Dolls

In some places, such as parts of Africa, children play with toys that they have made at home. Their families are too poor to buy toys from shops so they make toys from discarded materials. Some of these toys are very intricate. They vary from making models of helicopters to making simple rag dolls.

Making a Rag Doll

This rag doll is made from scraps of coloured fabric and wool. Make the head by cutting the 'foot' from a pair of nylon tights and stuffing it to make a ball shape. Cover the ball with a length of fabric, tying it tightly at the neck with yarn.

Roll up another length of fabric to make the arm shape, binding it with yarn at each end to form hands. Divide the fabric at the neck and tie the arms into place around the waist. This makes the basic doll-shape. Tuck extra fabric strips into the waist band.

Making the Doll

making the head

attaching the arms

dressing the doll

Worry Dolls

Children of Central America traditionally tell their troubles and worries to tiny dolls before going to sleep at night. These dolls are made from coloured threads. There is one doll for each worry. The dolls are placed beneath their pillows and while they are asleep the dolls solve all their problems.

Making a Pipe-cleaner Body

Make a Family of Worry Dolls and Keep Them in a Drawstring Bag

Making Worry Dolls

You can make your own worry dolls to tell your troubles to. Make the body structures from pipe-cleaners, twisting them into shape as shown here. Bind wool around the pipe-cleaners, using different colours for the features and clothes. Make a complete family and keep them in a little bag.

← drawstring bag

Glossary

Arachne A character from a Greek myth. Her weaving skills so enraged the jealous goddess Athena that she turned Arachne into a spider.

Bayeux Tapestry An embroidery 70 m long and 48 cm wide that tells the story of the Norman invasion of Britain in 1066.

Bunraku Style of puppetry that originated in the sixteenth century in Japan. The large string puppets need 3 puppeteers to operate them.

chindi Rags sorted into bundles by Hindu women and children, mainly in Ahmedabad in Gujarat, India. The rags are recycled in textile mills.

durable Able to last for a long time.

fabric Any cloth, woven or non-woven, made from yarn or fibres.

fibres Natural or synthetic filaments that can be spun into yarn.

flexible Able to bend easily without breaking.

garments Articles of clothing.

genetic engineering When humans interfere with nature by constructing and combining genes.

hem A folded raw edge on a piece of cloth, usually stitched down.

hessian A coarse jute fabric similar to sacking.

knitting A way of looping and entwining yarn with long eyeless needles to make shaped pieces of cloth.

loom A frame on which yarn is woven into cloth.

marionettes Puppets with jointed limbs worked by strings.

material Substance of which something is made.

panja looms Devices found in Indian homes and used to weave rag rugs.

remnant A piece of left-over fabric.

synthetic Describes an artificially-made material. The material is made by a chemical reaction.

taut Tightly stretched.

Tencel A brand new textile made from wood pulp and cotton.

threads Strands of material, usually fabric.

warp The lengthwise fixed threads on a loom.

weft Threads woven in and out across the lengthwise warp threads on a loom.

worsted Woollen fabric with a hard, smooth, close-textured surface.

yarn A continuous strand of fibres used in weaving and knitting.

More Information

Books to Read

Allen J. & Brown M., *The Last Green Book on Earth*, Red Fox, 1994

Bawden, Juliet, *Fun with Fabric*, Hamlyn, 1994

Crowe, Carol, *Craft Workshop: Fabric*, Crabtree Publishing, 1998

Inskipp, Carol, *Improving Our Environment: Waste and Recycling*, Wayland, 2005

Lancaster, John, *Fabric Art*, Franklin Watts, 1991

Martin, Laura C. *The Art of Recycling*, Storey Books, 2004

Addresses for Information

Australia

Australian Conservation Foundation, Floor 1, 60 Leicester Street, Carlton, Vic 3053

Canada

International Council for Local Environmental Initiatives, City Hall, West Tower, 16th Floor, 100 Queen St. Ontario M5H 2N2

UK

British Wool Marketing Board, Wool House, Roydsdale Way, Euroway Trading Estate, Bradford, West Yorkshire, BD4 6SE

Oakley Fabrics, 8 May Street, Luton, Beds, LU1 3QY

Places to Visit (UK)

British Museum, Great Russell Street, London WC1B 3DG

The Colour Museum (Textile Printing and Dyeing), 82 Gratton Road, Bradford BD1 2JB

Commonwealth Institute, 80 Haymarket, London SWIY 4TQ

Museum of London, 150 London Wall, EC2Y 5HN

Museum of Mankind, Burlington Gardens, W1X 2EX

Quarry Bank Mill (Museum of Cotton Industry), Styal, Wilmslow, Cheshire, SK9 4LA

Victoria and Albert Museum, Cromwell Road, South Kensington, SW7 2RL

Sources for Special Materials

Charity shops, jumble sales and the remnant sections of fabric shops.

History
1. Wool production in the Middle Ages/wool staple/domestic industry
2. Industrial Revolution/changes in textile production/factory labour/children in industry/20th century rug production in India
3. Flags and banners/Bayeux Tapestry
4. Costume and fashion through the ages
5. Slave trade/cotton plantations/trading triangle – Liverpool/West Africa/Caribbean

Art and Craft
1. Pattern and texture/collage
2. Spinning and weaving
3. Colours
4. Fabric printing/tie-dyeing/ batik/silk painting
5. Patchwork/plaiting/ puppets

Literature/ Language
1. Vocabulary of fabrics – fibre/thread/textile etc
2. Greek myths – Arachne
3. Folk tales of India
4. Puppet shows

Mathematics
1. Measuring, area
2. Direction

Topic Web Art from Fabric

Religious Education
1. Religious beliefs of many cultures

Design and Technology
1. Fashion design and creation, pattern making
2. Joints and levers marionettes
3. Structures/ puppet theatres/ balance and stability/kites/ windsocks

Geography
1. Industry/textiles/India/Shetlands/ plantation cultivation of fibres e.g cotton/pesticides and the environment/ sheep farming in Australia
2. Weather/wind direction/suitable clothing for cold or hot weather/ waterproofing
3. Environmental considerations/ pollution caused by industrial processes/bleaching/dioxins

Science
1. Human development and the environment – landfill sites/ pollution/deforestation
2. Ourselves – personal hygiene/keeping warm/keeping cool
3. Properties of materials – synthetic/natural fabrics – testing for strength, insulating properties, texture, elasticity, durability, strength, opacity, translucency
4. Changing the properties of materials combining materials/ weaving
5. Air/kites and windsocks

Index